COLOR BOISE

BOISE DEPOT

... a BOISE COLORING BOOK ...
by: Shelley Hodges

Spotting Zoo Giraffes from Greenbelt

Deer Visiting Warm Springs Golf Course

Homestead Trail Pronghorn

Birds of Prey Fall Flights

Spirit of Boise at Ann Morrison Park

Idanha Building

Sledding Simplot Hill

Harvesting a Christmas Forest Tree

Boise Whitewater Park

M.K. Nature Center Rainbow Trout

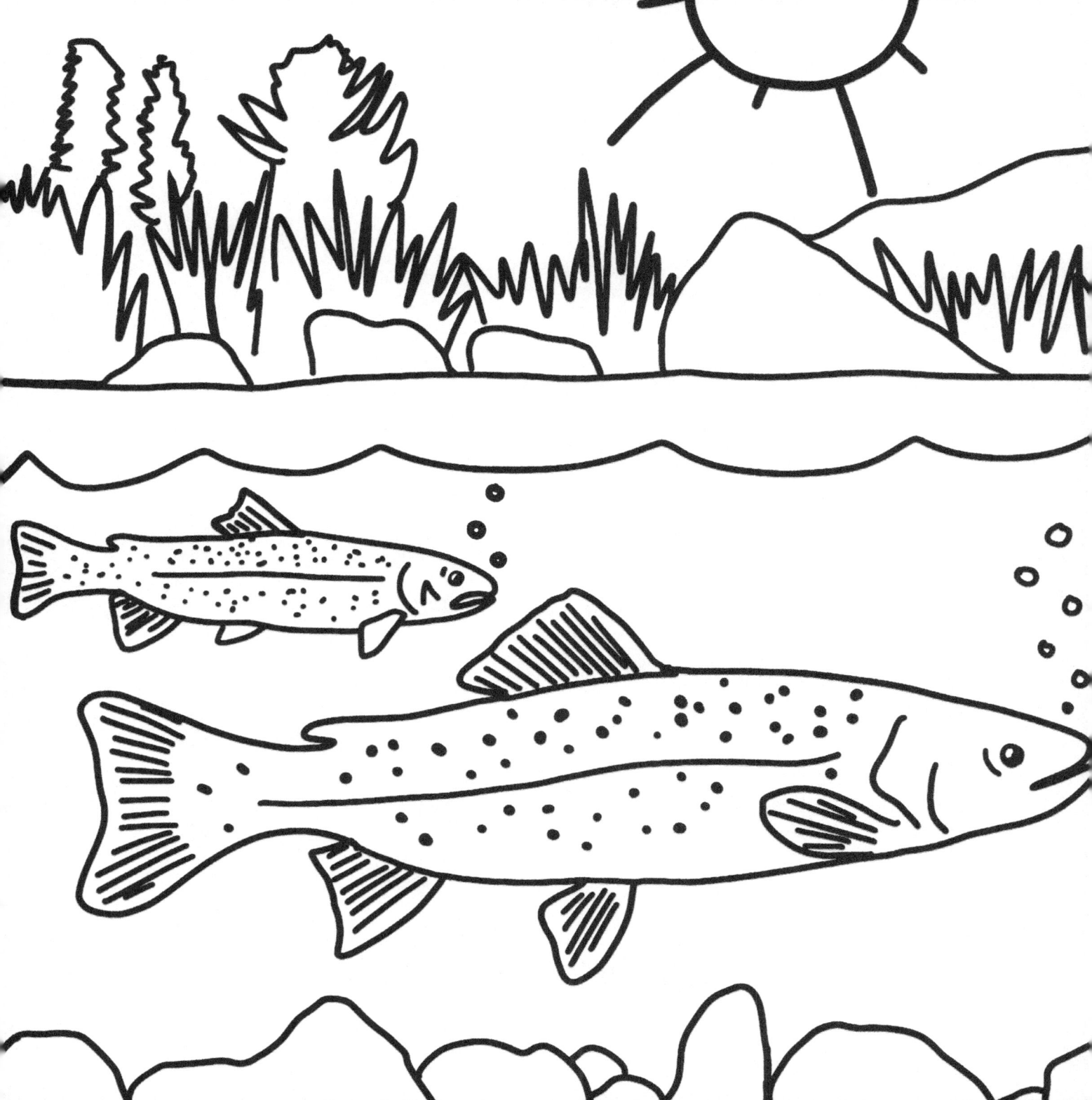

Paragliding Crow Hill

Climbing Black Cliffs

Arrowleaf Flowers in Bloom

Capital City Public Market

Egyptian Theater

Lucky Peak Boating

Skateboard Loving Dog

Richard the Coffee Mule

Sheep Grazing the Foothills

Backcountry Flying

Table Rock

Biking the Greenbelt

Floating the Boise River

Boise Depot

Boise River Bald Eagle

Diversion Dam

Camel's Back Park

Valley Construction

Skiing Bogus Basin

Lucky Peak State Park Paddle Boarding

Idaho Capitol

Ernie the Elk Amongst Cattle

Idaho Penitentiary

Boise on the Map

Basque Block Paella

Idaho Shakespeare Festival

J.U.M.P. Slide

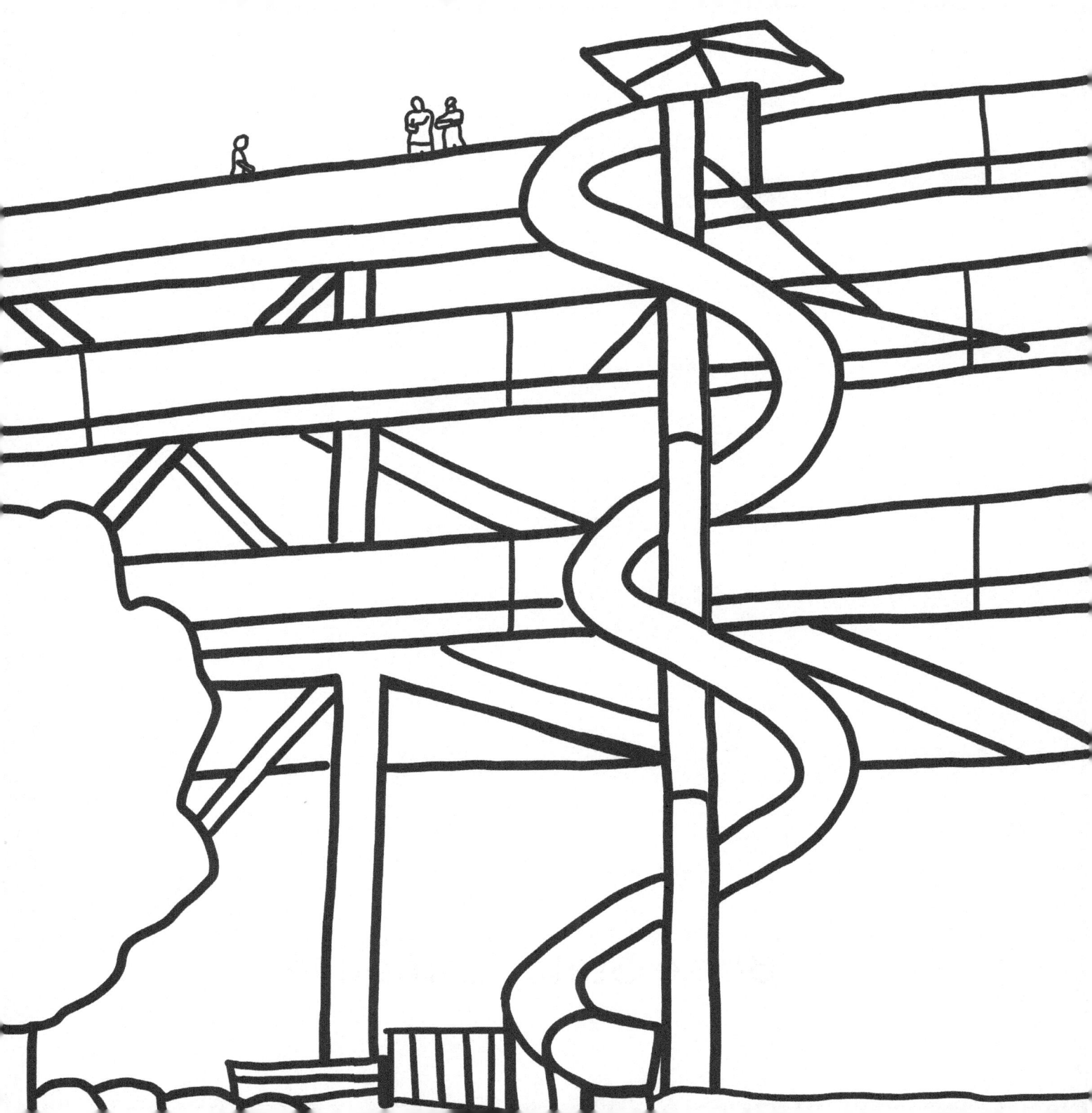

Boise State Game Day

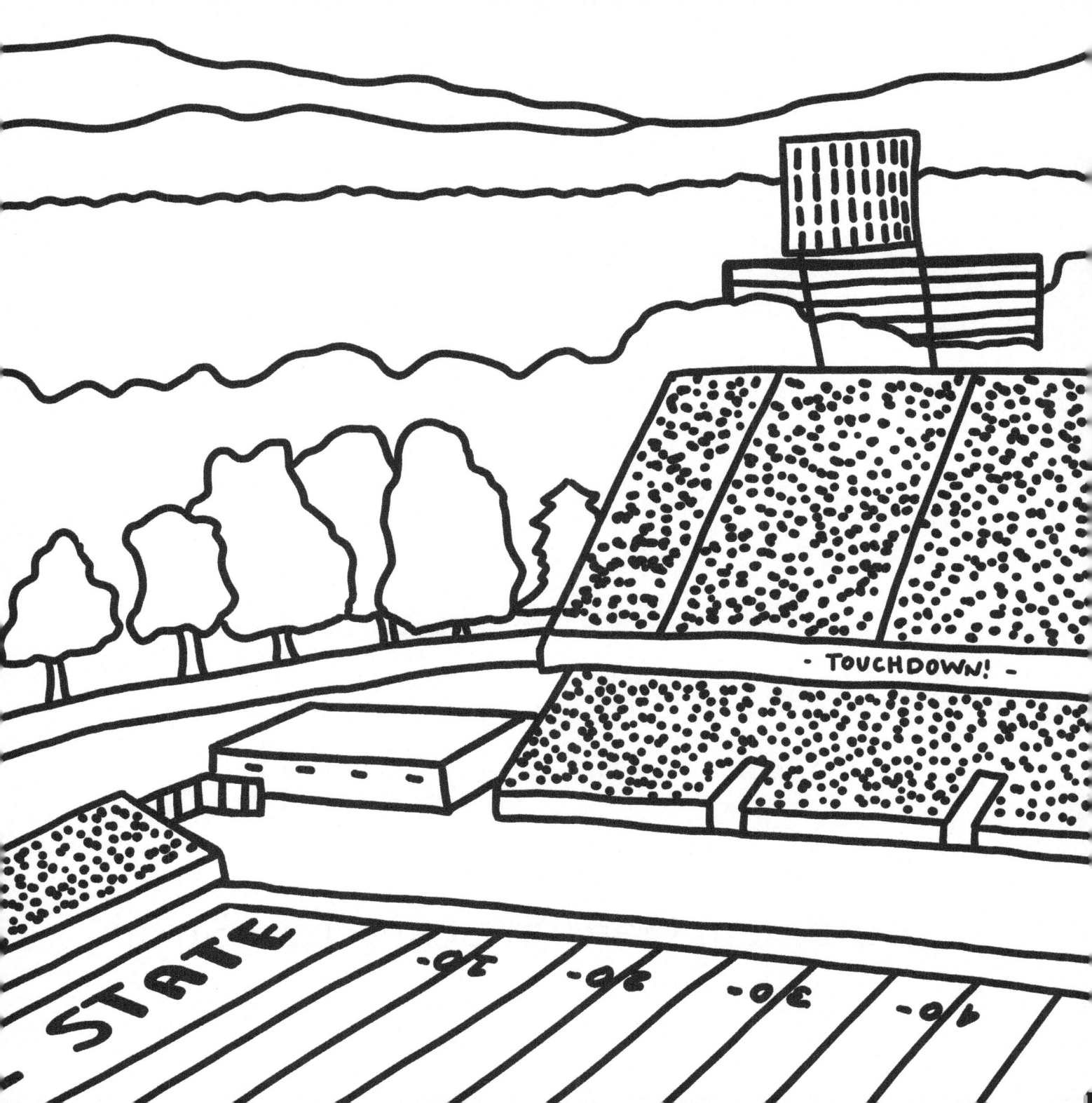

Botanical Garden Scarecrow Stroll

Cheri Buckner-Webb Park

Boise Bicycle Park

Freak Alley

Draw Your Favorite Boise Destination

ABOUT:

Shelley is a painter who started drawing due to repeated requests from her toddler. She created Color Boise as a way for her Idaho kids and others far and near to explore this wonderful city they call home. Most of the scenes are inspired by her family's favorite memories and places.

Thank you to my friends and family for the encouragement,
support, and motivation to make this dream a reality!

ISBN: 979 8 61651 629 9

www.ColorBoise.com
Instagram.com/ColorBoise
Facebook.com/ColorBoise

Made in the USA
Middletown, DE
26 July 2024

57855572R00051